DEBUGGING
YOU CAN FIX IT!

Lyrics by PATRICIA M. STOCKLAND
Illustrations by SR. SÁNCHEZ
Music by MARK MALLMAN

CANTATA
LEARNING

WWW.CANTATALEARNING.COM

CANTATA LEARNING

Published by Cantata Learning
1710 Roe Crest Drive
North Mankato, MN 56003
www.cantatalearning.com

Library of Congress Cataloging-in-Publication Data
Names: Stockland, Patricia M., author. | Sánchez, Sr., 1973– illustrator. |
  Mallman, Mark, composer.
Title: Debugging : you can fix it! / Lyrics by Patricia M. Stockland ;
  illustrations by Sr. Sánchez ; music by Mark Mallman.
Description: North Mankato, MN : Cantata Learning, 2018. | Series: Code it! |
  Audience: Ages 6–9. | Audience: K to grade 3.
Identifiers: LCCN 2017017547 (print) | LCCN 2017047500 (ebook) | ISBN
  9781684101528 (ebook) | ISBN 9781684101450 (hardcover : alk. paper)
Subjects: LCSH: Repairing--Juvenile literature. | Problem solving--Juvenile
  literature. | Debugging in computer science--Juvenile literature. |
  Railroads--Models--Maintenance and repair--Juvenile literature.
Classification: LCC TT151 (ebook) | LCC TT151 .S745 2018 (print) | DDC
  643/.7--dc23
LC record available at https://lccn.loc.gov/2017017547

Book design and art direction, Tim Palin Creative
Editorial direction, Kellie M. Hultgren
Music direction, Elizabeth Draper
Music arranged and produced by Mark Mallman

Printed in the United States of America in North Mankato, Minnesota.
122017   0378CGS18

ACCESS THE MUSIC!
SCAN CODE WITH MOBILE APP
CANTATALEARNING.COM

TIPS TO SUPPORT LITERACY AT HOME

WHY READING AND SINGING WITH YOUR CHILD IS SO IMPORTANT

Daily reading with your child leads to increased academic achievement. Music and songs, specifically rhyming songs, are a fun and easy way to build early literacy and language development. Music skills correlate significantly with both phonological awareness and reading development. Singing helps build vocabulary and speech development. And reading and appreciating music together is a wonderful way to strengthen your relationship.

READ AND SING EVERY DAY!

TIPS FOR USING CANTATA LEARNING BOOKS AND SONGS DURING YOUR DAILY STORY TIME

1. As you sing and read, point out the different words on the page that rhyme. Suggest other words that rhyme.

2. Memorize simple rhymes such as Itsy Bitsy Spider and sing them together. This encourages comprehension skills and early literacy skills.

3. Use the questions in the back of each book to guide your singing and storytelling.

4. Read the included sheet music with your child while you listen to the song. How do the music notes correlate to the words of the song?

5. Sing along on the go and at home. Access music by scanning the QR code on each Cantata book. You can also stream or download the music for free to your computer, smartphone, or mobile device.

Devoting time to daily reading shows that you are available for your child. Together, you are building language, literacy, and listening skills.

Have fun reading and singing!

How do you find and fix a problem? **Debugging** is one way. When you debug something, you go step by step until you see where something goes wrong. Then you can fix the step that doesn't work. Codes are sets of **directions** to get things done. What if the directions don't work? You can debug them too.

Follow along to see what's wrong with the train set. Sing the song to help debug the problem!

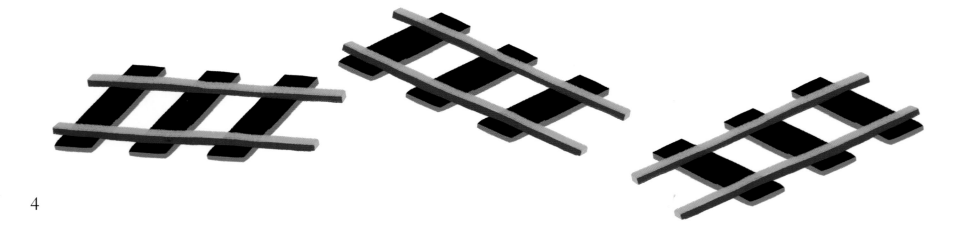

Our train set isn't working!
The **engine** just won't go.

It's stuck on the track. There's no clickety-clack.
We need to check high and low.

We can debug our problem.
Something is out of whack.

Step by step, we check and test
to get things back on track.

First we'll check the engine.

The **battery** is a-okay.

The wheels are fine. They're all in line.

This isn't the problem today.

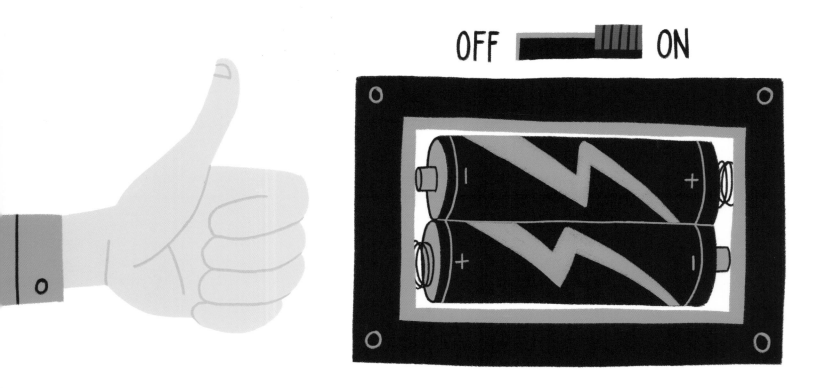

11

We can debug our problem.
Something is out of whack.

Step by step, we check and test
to get things back on track.

DIRECTIONS
1.
2.
3.
4.

Next we'll check the rail cars.

They're all hooked up in a line.

The wheels all turn. What did we learn?

This part seems just fine.

We can debug our problem.
Something is out of whack.

Step by step, we check and test
to get things back on track.

Last, we'll check the rail lines.
Is everything **attached**?

The rails don't meet! The problem is beat.
We fixed it just like that!

19

We have debugged our problem!
Something was out of whack.

Step by step, we check and test
and get things back on track.

SONG LYRICS
Debugging: You Can Fix It!

Our train set isn't working!
The engine just won't go.
It's stuck on the track. There's no clickety-
   clack.
We need to check high and low.

We can debug our problem.
Something is out of whack.
Step by step, we check and test
to get things back on track.

First we'll check the engine.
The battery is a-okay.
The wheels are fine. They're all in line.
This isn't the problem today.

We can debug our problem.
Something is out of whack.
Step by step, we check and test
to get things back on track.

Next we'll check the rail cars.
They're all hooked up in a line.
The wheels all turn. What did we learn?
This part seems just fine.

We can debug our problem.
Something is out of whack.
Step by step, we check and test
to get things back on track.

Last, we'll check the rail lines.
Is everything attached?
The rails don't meet! The problem is beat.
We fixed it just like that!

We have debugged our problem!
Something was out of whack.
Step by step, we check and test
and get things back on track.

Debugging: You Can Fix It!

Funky Electro Pop
Mark Mallman

Verse

1. Our train set is-n't work-ing! The en-gine just won't go. It's stuck on the track. There's no click-e-ty-clack.

We need to check high and low.

Chorus

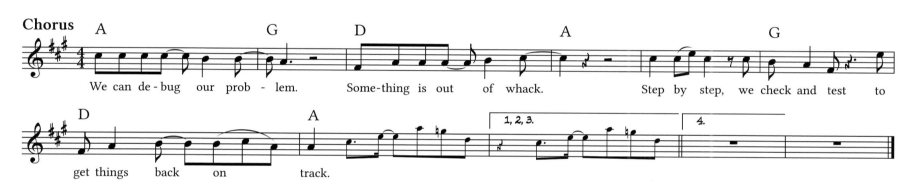

We can de-bug our prob-lem. Some-thing is out of whack. Step by step, we check and test to

get things back on track.

Verse 2
First we'll check the engine.
The battery is a-okay.
The wheels are fine. They're all in line.
This isn't the problem today.

Chorus

Verse 3
Next we'll check the rail cars.
They're all hooked up in a line.
The wheels all turn. What did we learn?
This part seems just fine.

Chorus

Verse 4
Last, we'll check the rail lines.
Is everything attached?
The rails don't meet! The problem is beat.
We fixed it just like that!

Chorus
We have debugged our problem!
Something was out of whack.
Step by step, we check and test
and get things back on track.

GLOSSARY

attached–to be joined together

battery–a source of power, which helps something move or operate

debugging–finding and fixing problems

directions–steps that tell how something should be done

engine–a machine with parts that move; on a train, the engine is the locomotive, which turns energy into power that moves the engine and any attached cars

GUIDED READING ACTIVITIES

1. What was wrong with the train set in the story? Which things did the kids check to find the problem?

2. Think of a time when something of yours wasn't working. What steps did you take to check the problem? Were you able to find the problem? Could you fix it?

3. *Debugging* is a funny word! What other words can you think of for following steps to find and fix a problem? Can you make up your own funny word for this?

TO LEARN MORE

Hubbard, Ben. *How Coding Works*. North Mankato, MN: Heinemann-Raintree. 2017.

Liukas, Linda. *Hello Ruby: Adventures in Coding*. New York: Feiwel and Friends, 2015.

Lyons, Heather, and Elizabeth Tweedale. *Coding, Bugs, and Fixes*. Minneapolis: Lerner, 2017.